BY STEAMER TO
THE AYRSHIRE COAST

ALISTAIR DEAYTON

AMBERLEY

come to the
CLYDECOAST
SCOTLAND'S HOLIDAY WONDERLAND

BOATING · SAILING · FISHING · WATER SKI-ING · GOLF · SEA ANGLING · CRUISING
YACHTING · SHOOTING · PONY TREKKING · MOUNTAINEERING · WALKING · SWIMMING

The cover for a late 1960s holiday brochure for the Clyde Coast, depicting the Glasgow Corporation sludge steamer *Shieldhall*, passing the Cloch Lighthouse on her return journey from depositing her load of sewage sludge off Garroch Head.

First published 2013

Amberley Publishing
The Hill, Stroud
Gloucestershire, GL5 4EP

www.amberley-books.com

British Library Cataloguing in Publication Data.
A catalogue record for this book is available from the British Library.

ISBN 978 1 4456 1286 7
eBook ISBN 978 1 4456 1307 9

Typeset in 10pt on 13pt Sabon.
Typesetting and Origination by Amberley Publishing.
Printed in the UK.

Introduction

This volume covers steamers that ran to and from the southern and eastern shores of the Clyde Coast from Greenock down as far as Stranraer. In addition, those that served the islands of Bute, Cumbrae, Arran and Ailsa Craig are covered.

We shall look at the steamers that ran both to and from the coastal resorts and towns, such as from the Inverclyde piers at Greenock, Gourock and Wemyss Bay, the North Ayrshire towns of Largs, Fairlie and Ardrossan, the South Ayrshire ports of Troon, Ayr and Girvan, not forgetting the islands of Bute, Cumbrae and Arran, and including evening cruises to some smaller uninhabited islands.

Sir Waiter Scott wrote in *The Heart of Midlothian* of the Clyde coast, written in 1819 and quoted in a North British Railway holiday guide-book published in 1905:

> The Islands in the Firth of Clyde, which the daily passage of so many smoke-pennoned steamboats now renders so easily accessible, were, in our father's time, secluded spots, frequented by no travellers, and few visitants of any kind. They are of exquisite, yet varied beauty. Arran, a mountainous region, or Alpine island, abounds with the grandeur and most romantic scenery. Bute is of a softer and more woodland character. The Cumbraes, as if to exhibit a contrast to both, are green, level and bare forming the links of a sort of natural bar, which is drawn along the mouth of the Firth, leaving large intervals, however, of ocean.

The places covered varied from the traditional seaside resorts of Largs, Ayr and Rothesay, with their beaches and amusement arcades, to the Arran villages, where mountain-climbing was a much more common activity for the visitor than sea-bathing. The Ayrshire Coast, like the Argyllshire coast, was the destination for long day excursions, and for shorter evening cruises, most of which did not give the traveller an opportunity to land at the advertised destinations.

Acknowledgements

The vast majority of the illustrations in this volume are from the author's own collection. Thanks are offered to the Clyde River Steamer Club for use of its archive collection of 1920s and 1930s handbills, and for the use of photographs produced by them over several decades. The author thanks Iain Quinn for checking the text for accuracy and for help in identifying the locations of some photos.

Inverclyde

Glasgow Central Station and Hotel in a postcard view, posted in 1904. Train services to Gourock and Wemyss Bay departed from here. The view is little changed today.

Greenock Custom House Quay was the traditional departure point at Greenock for steamers to the coast, seen here in this mid-Victorian engraving. It is still used today by the paddle steamer *Waverley*.

Greenock Custom House Quay with the GSWR steamer *Minerva* approaching. It was still used even after the railway company had opened Princes Pier in 1894, up until 1915, being close to the town centre.

Right: The West India Harbour at Greenock, showing a paddle tug, in a postcard view posted in January 1906.

Below: *Waverley* berthed at Greenock Custom House Quay on 8 July 2012.

Greenock Princes Pier had an ornate building in the Italianate style, with railway platforms at a higher level than the pier. It is seen here in a postcard view with *Mars*, the final GSWR paddle steamer to be built. The pier buildings should have been a candidate for preservation, but were demolished in 1967 to make way for the container terminal.

Greenock Princes Pier seen from the east, with the GSWR's *Marquis of Bute* berthed and the Lochgoil Company's *Windsor Castle* departing, with a NB steamer berthed in the distance.

The regular steamer service to Princes Pier ceased in 1959, although special trains for the Cunard and Canadian Pacific liners lasted until 1965. Latterly it was used as a mooring point for tugs, as seen here in a shot from the early 1960s, showing a Clyde Shipping Co. tug. The station was demolished in 1967 and the site was used for the Greenock Container Terminal. This is where cruise ships now berth on their visits to the Clyde.

Gourock Pier was opened on 1 June 1889 by the Caledonian Railway and soon developed into the most important departure point for the Clyde Steamers. It is seen here from Lyle hill in a Tuck's 'Oilette' postcard in the 'Clyde Watering Places' series. Two steamers can be seen, one at the pier and one in mid-Firth.

The Caledonian Steam Packet's paddle steamer *Caledonia* departing Gourock in a postcard view taken after 1911, when her bridge was moved forward of the funnel.

The CSP steamer *Galatea* at Gourock Pier in an Edwardian postcard view taken prior to 1906, when she was sold to Italian owners.

The 1937 *Jupiter* berthed at Gourock in the 1950s and dressed overall, flying the British India Steam Navigation Co. house flag, probably for a corporate charter, with a coach on the pier, which had most likely brought the passengers there.

Jeanie Deans at Gourock Pier *c.* 1950, taken from the upper deck of *Waverley*.

The relief Ardrishaig mail steamer *Lochnevis* at Gourock in the 1960s with a Maid class vessel just visible further along the pier.

The Kilcreggan ferry and cruise vessel *Seabus* at what remains of Gourock Pier in April 2010.

The Holy Loch vessel *Maid of Ashton* berthed at Gourock in the 1960s, with sister vessel *Maid of Skelmorlie* lying out of use 'at the wires' further along the pier.

A rather faded postcard view of Gourock from Lyle Road, posted in 1908 and showing two CSP steamers berthed at the pier and one arriving, and five steam yachts moored in Cardwell Bay amongst the sailing yachts.

A Second World War postcard entitled 'The last convoy', showing a large number of ships, with a three-funnelled liner also visible, heading down-firth at the start of a transatlantic convoy, heading for the USA or Canada, with Gourock Pier in the foreground.

From Tower Hill.   *Gourock.*

Gourock from more westerly vantage point, Tower Hill, seen here in an Edwardian postcard view with only the rear of the pier buildings visible.

Ashton is the seaside end of Gourock, seen here in this Edwardian postcard view of the 'New Yacht Pond'.

A later view of the same location, now entitled 'Children's Boating Pond'.

Gourock has been notable for yachting for many years, with a regatta seen off Ashton in the early years of the twentieth century in this postcard view

Shore Street, Gourock, showing the tramlines and shops in a postcard view printed in Berlin.

A distorted view of Kempock Street, Gourock, entitled 'How we saw Kempock Street, Gourock, after a glorious spree'.

The war memorial and Albert Road, Gourock, with a tram in the distance, in a postcard view posted in 1925. The Greenock & Port Glasgow Tramway Co. operated horse teams from Port Glasgow to Ashton from 1873 to 1901 and electric trams from 1901 until replaced by buses in July 1929.

Cloch Lighthouse, Gourock   RELIABLE SERIES 827

The Cloch Lighthouse, at the point where the Firth of Clyde opens out and the coastline turns southward, on a Reliable Series postcard.

An Edwardian postcard of the thatched-roofed pilot cottage at the Cloch Point posted in August 1905.

The railway from Port Glasgow to Wemyss Bay was opened in 1865, along with the pier at Wemyss Bay. That is seen here, with, clockwise from the left, the steamers *Largs*, *Lancelot*, *Lady Gertrude*, and *Argyle*.

In 1903 a magnificent new station and pier was opened, which survives to this day.

The covered walkway from the station to the pier at Wemyss Bay. The station was refurbished and returned to its original condition in recent years and is now looked after by the support group The Friends of Wemyss Bay Station.

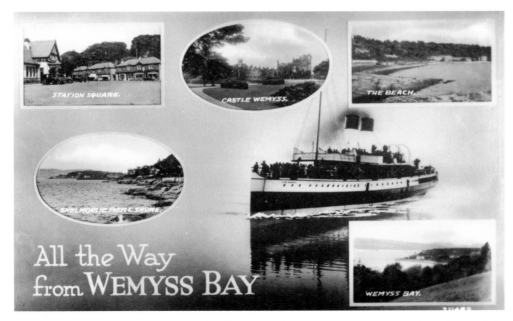

A sepia multi-view postcard entitled 'All the way from WEMYSS BAY', with a photo of the turbine steamer *King Edward*, which never called there in regular service after her initial years of operation.

Wemyss Bay had two main berths; the northerly, to the left, for Rothesay, and the southerly for Largs, Millport (Old Pier) and Kilchattan Bay. Here the *Marchioness of Lorne* is seen at the Rothesay berth and the *Marchioness of Bute* at the Millport berth.

Mercury at the Rothesay berth at Wemyss Bay between 1925 and 1933.

Left: A unique semaphore signalling tower was located at the seaward end of Wemyss Bay Pier, seen here in the 1960s.

Below: Marchioness of Breadalbane at the Millport berth at Wemyss Bay in an Edwardian postcard view.

The car ferry *Bute* at the south side of Wemyss Bay pier in 1964 or earlier, on the thrice weekly car ferry service to Millport. This is the location of the present Rothesay car ferry berth.

Wemyss Bay pier as it is today. It has been shortened somewhat, as has the covered walkway, after a fire in 1977.

A replica of an African hut used by David Livingstone was built in the grounds of Kelly House at Wemyss Bay in 1875, which was owned by James 'Paraffin' Young, who was a friend of Livingstone.

A view of the Old Mill, Kelly Glen, in the hills behind Wemyss Bay. Wemyss Bay and its neighbour, Skelmorlie, just over the border into Ayrshire, never really developed as holiday destinations.

North Ayrshire

Largs was a call for steamers from Glasgow to Millport up until ten years before the railway was opened to there in 1885, the steamers then running from Wemyss Bay. In the 1950s and early 60s a shuttle service to Millport was maintained by the small motor vessels *Ashton* and *Leven*, one of which is seen here at Largs with the turbine *Marchioness of Graham* at the pier in a mid-1960s view.

From 1967 to 1986, the Millport vessel was the former Tilbury to Gravesend ferry *Keppel*, seen with the ABC car ferry *Bute*, which made a thrice-weekly sailing to Millport with cars and commercial vehicles.

Above left: A handbill for an evening cruise to Largs Fair from the Gareloch piers, Helensburgh and Kilcreggan by the LNER steamer *Waverley* on 16 June 1925.

Above right: A handbill for evening cruises from Rothesay and Craigmore by Williamson-Buchanan Steamers' *Kylemore* on the same evening and the previous evening

Largs Old Pier in the early years of the twenty-first century with *Waverley* berthed at low tide.

Largs Pier was rebuilt in 2008-9, with a longer face to enable the Cumbrae ferry *Loch Shira* to berth there overnight.

Largs Esplanade has been a favourite place to hire rowing boats or motorboats since the early years of the twentieth century, as seen in this postcard view, posted in 1920.

The Esplanade at Largs seen from the pier in an Edwardian postcard view. The drawback of hiring motorboats was that there was no fuel gauge and the author remembers having to row back from near Cumbrae after the fuel ran out.

A similar view taken in recent years showing Nardini's café, which has been a favourite destination for ice creams such as Knickerbocker Glories since 1935.

Large Esplanade in a Raphael Tuck's 'Oilette' postcard view, another of the 'Clyde Watering Places' series.

Largs Esplanade from the north with a GSWR steamer at the pier in another Raphael Tuck postcard, this time from the 'Rapholette Glossy' series, posted in August 1913.

South of the pier there is a model yacht sailing pond, still used today by local modellers.

Largs Main Street in a postcard view posted in London in November 1908.

The Moorings Café at the Pier Head was always the great competitor to Nardini's, although now it has been rebuilt and is owned by the Nardini family, while the large café has been sold to another company, although retaining the name Nardini.

Largs Main Street looking towards the pier in a postcard view so detailed that the registration numbers of two cars can be read.

LARGS FROM THE AIR.

B.6937.
"SCOTTISH DAILY MAIL PHOTO."

Largs from the air in a postcard with the caption 'Scottish Daily Mail Photo', with the *Duchess of Fife* arriving from Millport in a post-1948 shot.

Fairlie Pier was used by the Campbeltown excursion steamers, and also for sailings to Millport and to Arran in the winter months. The GSWR's *Marquis of Bute* is seen there between 1893 and 1895 when she was on the Fairlie to Millport service.

The Arran car ferry *Glen Sannox* at Fairlie in the 1965 to 1969 Monastral Blue hull colours.

The *Maid of Ashton* departing Fairlie for Millport in the late 1960s.

Fairlie village in an old postcard view. Fairlie was never really a popular holiday destination and was more noted for the yachts built by the yard of William Fyfe.

Portencross, then spelt 'Portincross', in a postcard view posted in 1905 and postmarked both Seamill and West Kilbride. A pier was built there in 1912, but saw only two years' service, mainly for excursions, until the outbreak of war made it redundant.

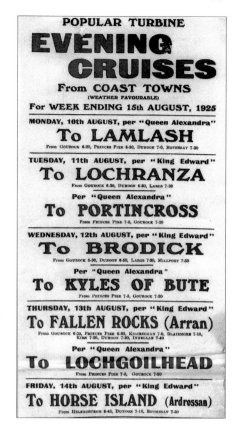

Right: A handbill for evening cruises by Turbine Steamers Ltd showing steamers for the week ending 15 August 1925, including one to Portincross (non-landing) from Princes Pier, and Gourock by *Queen Alexandra*.

Below: On 16 April 1995, Easter Sunday, *Waverley* made a unique call at Portencross on a special sailing.

Left: Ardrossan (Winton Pier) was the Glasgow & South Western Railway railhead for the sailings to Arran, and is seen here around 1960. There were occasional pick-up calls here by the Ayr excursion steamer.

Below: Ferry *Isle of Arran* departing Ardrossan for Brodick on 25 May 2013.

Saltcoats has a small harbour, little used in the steam age and never by Clyde steamers. It is seen here in a postcard view posted in 1905 with four sail and oar-powered fishing boats lying in the harbour. Saltcoats was also a favoured destination of Glasgow people in the days before cheap flights to the Spanish Costas.

Irvine has rarely been a port of call for Clyde Steamers, although it was a regular lay-up berth for some. *Waverley* called there on 22 August 1978 on a cruise from Ayr, Largs, Millport and Brodick and on 21 August 1979 en route from Ayr to Campbeltown. This is the timetable for the 1978 trip.

TUESDAY AUGUST 22.		
AYR	dep.	0730
Millport	dep.	0915
Largs		0945
Brodick		1115
Irvine	dep.	1300
CRUISE		
Irvine	arr.	1500
	dep.	1530
Brodick		1645
Millport		1800
Largs		1830
Ayr	arr.	2030

South Ayrshire

Troon was a call on most excursion sailings over the years from Ayr by *Neptune*, *Juno*, *Duchess of Hamilton*, *Marchioness of Graham* and *Caledonia*. *Juno* is seen here entering the harbour

The GSWR's *Juno* berthed at Troon harbour in a postcard view posted in 1903. She was the Ayr-based excursion steamer all her life, from 1898 until 1931, with the exception of the war years from 1915 until 1919.

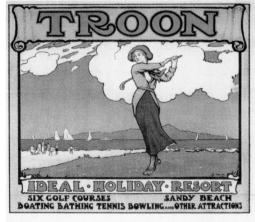

Above: Juno, berthed at Troon in her 1923 colours, with the 'tartan lum' and GSWR grey hull, is in the centre of this multi-view card of Troon, with the other images portraying the Esplanade, the beach, Portland Street, the main shopping street, and the municipal golf course and clubhouse.

Right: Troon in a joint GSWR/Midland Railway poster featuring a lady golfer.

Left: Edwardian families on Troon
Esplanade in a postcard view, posted in May
1910.

Below: Troon Harbour in a postcard view,
posted in July 1903.

A copy of a poster for the paddle steamer *Bonnie Doon* from around 1880. She ran from Glasgow to Ayr at 7 a.m. daily, calling at Greenock, Kirn, Dunoon, Largs, Millport, Ardrossan and Troon. She replaced an earlier steamer of the same name and operated on the route from building in 1876 until 1880, when she was sold to operate in North Wales, finally being scrapped in 1913 after a peripatetic career round the English and Welsh Coast.

Troon Harbour in a 1950s postcard view with the puffer *Spartan*, now preserved at the Scottish Maritime Museum in Irvine, lying outside *Roman*, with a third puffer, *Sealight*, in the background.

Ayr Pier

SPECIAL PLEASURE EXCURSIONS
To AYR,
Calling at LARGS and MILLPORT,
On MONDAYS, 6th, 13th, 20th & 27th JULY,
By Saloon Steamer "NEPTUNE."

(Train leaves St. Enoch at 8-45 a.m.)

as under:—   RETURN JOURNEY.

				a.m.						p.m.
Greenock, Princes Pier,		dep.	9 40	Ayr, ..	..	..	..	dep.	3 30
Dunoon, ..	..	..	,,	10 0	Millport,	..	..	..	,,	5 0
Innellan,	..	..	,,	10 15	Largs,	..	..	..	,,	5 25
Rothesay,	..	..	,,	10 45	Craigmore,	..	..	..	,,	5 50
Craigmore, ..	..	..	,,	10 50	Rothesay,	..	..	..	,,	6 0
Largs,	..	..	,,	11 15	Innellan,	..	..	..	,,	6 25
Millport,	..	..	,,	11 35	Dunoon,	..	..	..	,,	6 40
Ayr, ..	..	..	arr.	1 0p	Princes Pier,	..	..	..	arr.	7 10
					Greenock,	..	..	Train dep.	7 25

Passengers have ample time to drive to and from Burns Monument.

Messrs. Gemmell & Sons intimate that their Coaches will await the Steamer's arrival at Ayr.

(For Circular Tour, returning from Ayr by Train, see page 12.)

RETURN FARES.

		SALOON.	FORE-SALOON.
From GREENOCK to AYR, ..	.. ..	2/3	1/6
,, ,, to LARGS or MILLPORT, ..	.. ..	1 6	1/
,, DUNOON, INNELLAN, & ROTHESAY to AYR,	.. ..	2/6	1/6
,, LARGS or MILLPORT to AYR, ..	.. .. ..	2/	1/6

Above: Neptune of the GSWR, which ran from Greenock Princes Pier to Ayr from the mid-1890s to 1906, entering Ayr harbour.

Left: The timetable for the cruise to Ayr by *Neptune* on Mondays in the July 1896 GSWR steamer timetable.

WEDNESDAYS.

21st AUGUST.

To COLINTRAIVE (Kyles of Bute), Passing LOCH RIDDEN,

Calling at KAMES and TIGHNABRUAICH, via ARRAN (Brodick only), as under—

Outward Journey.			a.m.		*Inward Journey.*			p.m.
Ayr,	..	dep.	10 0	Colintraive,	..	dep.	3 0
Troon,	..	,,	10 30	Tighnabruaich,	..	,,	3 20
Ardrossan,	..	,,	11 5	Kames,	..	,,	3 30
Brodick,	..	,,	11 55	Brodick,	..	,,	4 40
Kames,	..	,,	1 15p	Ardrossan,	..	,,	5 30
Tighnabruaich,	..	,,	1 15	Troon,	..	,,	6 5
Colintraive,	..	arr. abt.	1 35	Ayr,	..	arr. abt.	6 35

RETURN FARES.

	Cabin.	Steerage.
Ayr, Troon, or Ardrossan to Colintraive,	3/	2/
Brodick to Colintraive,	2/	1/6
Ayr or Troon to Brodick,	2/	1/6

COACH DRIVES IN CONNECTION. { Passengers have time to drive from Kames to Ardlamont and back, or from Colintraive to Loch Striven and back. Return Coach Fare, for either Drive, 1/.

28th AUGUST.

To KYLES OF BUTE (COLINTRAIVE, TIGHNABRUAICH, and KAMES), via ROTHESAY, as under—

Outward Journey.			a.m.		*Inward Journey.*			p.m.
Ayr,	..	dep.	10 0	Kames,	..	dep.	2 55
Troon,	..	,,	10 30	Tighnabruaich,	..	,,	3 5
Ardrossan,	..	,,	11 5	Colintraive,	..	,,	3 20
Keppel Pier (Millport),	,,	11 45	Rothesay,	..	,,	3 50
Largs,	..	,,	12 0n	Largs,	..	,,	4 20
Rothesay,	..	,,	12 30p	Keppel Pier (Millport),	,,	4 35
Colintraive,	..	,,	1 0	Ardrossan,	..	arr. abt.	5 35
Tighnabruaich,	..	rr. abt.	1 15	Troon,	..	,,	5 50
Kames,	..	,,	1 25	Ayr,	..	,,	6 20

RETURN FARES.

	Cabin.	Steerage.
Ayr, Troon, or Ardrossan to Kyles of Bute,	3/	2/
Ayr or Troon to Millport or Largs,	2/6	2/
Ardrossan to Rothesay,	2/	1/6
Millport or Largs to Kyles of Bute,	2/	1/6
Rothesay to Kyles of Bute,	1/6	1/

Passengers have time to drive from Kames to Ardlamont and back, or from Colintraive to Loch Striven and back. Return Coach Fare, for either Drive, 1/.

4th SEPTEMBER.

To ARROCHAR (Loch Long) for Loch Lomond.

Outward Journey.			a.m.		*Inward Journey.*			p.m.
Ayr,	..	dep	10 0	Arrochar,	..	dep.	3 15
Troon,	..	,,	10 30	Largs,	..	,,	5 0
Ardrossan,	..	,,	11 5	Keppel Pier (Millport),	,,	5 15
Keppel Pier (Millport),	,,	11 45	Ardrossan,	..	arr. abt.	5 55
Largs,	..	,,	12 0n	Troon,	..	,,	6 30
Arrochar,	..	arr. abt.	1 45p	Ayr,	..	,,	7 0

RETURN FARES.

	Cabin.	Steerage.
Ayr, Troon, or Ardrossan to Arrochar,	3/	2/
Ayr or Troon to Millport or Largs,	2/6	2/
Millport or Largs to Arrochar,	2/6	2/

Allowing Passengers time to drive to and from Loch Lomond. Return Coach Fare, 1/.

EVENING CRUISES } Are advertised during the Season from AYR and TROON. See separate Posters and page 39 of Programme.

30

Right: A selection of cruises by *Juno* from Ayr, Troon and Ardrossan on Wednesdays in August and September 1901 to Colintraive via the west of Bute, to the three Kyles of Bute piers via Rothesay, and to Arrochar.

Below: *Juno* berthed at Ayr, with the turbine steamer *Glen Sannox* lying behind her on a summer Sunday in 1925. *Juno* was the Ayr excursion steamer from building in 1898 until 1931.

SPECIAL SAILINGS

On 18th, 19th & 20th July

LUXURIOUS STEAMER

"QUEEN-EMPRESS"

TO

LARGS. MILLPORT

AND

AYR

(Weather Favourable)

From DUNOON at 10-20 a.m.

DIRECT TO LARGS, MILLPORT & AYR

Returning from AYR at 4.15 p.m.; MILLPORT, 6.0 p.m.; LARGS, 8.20 p.m
DUE DUNOON, 7.0 p.m.

Passengers can have about 6 Hours at Largs or Millport
or 3 Hours at Ayr.

RETURN FARES FROM DUNOON:

LARGS or **MILLPORT** - Saloon 2/-   Fore-Saloon 1/6

AYR - - - - do. **4/-**   do.   **3/-**

JOHN WILLIAMSON & CO., 99 Great Clyde Street, Glasgow, C.1.

A handbill for sailings to Ayr by *Queen-Empress* in July 1927 from Largs and Millport.

TO AYR

(via Brodick)

By T.S. "DUCHESS OF HAMILTON"

FRIDAYS (Ceases after 11th September)

OUTWARD				RETURN		
TRAIN	a.m.	a.m.	a.m.	**STEAMER**		p.m.
Glasgow (Central) lve.	—	7R 40	8 30	Ayr ... ... lve.		4 10
Glasgow (Qu. St.) ,,	7R 44	—	—	Brodick ... ... arr.		5 25
Paisley (Gil. St.) ,,	—	7A 54	8 44	Millport (Keppel Pier) ,,		6 15
Port Glasgow ... ,,	—	8 25	9 7	Largs ... ... ,,		6 30
Greenock (Cen.) ,,	—	8 34	9U 17	Rothesay ... ... ,,		7 5
Greenock (West) ,,	—	8 38	—	Wemyss Bay ... ... ,,		8R 15
Singer ... ... ,,	8R 5	—	—			
Dumbarton (Cen.) ,,	8R 19	—	—	Dunoon ... ... ,,		7 45
Craigendoran ... arr.	8 32	—	—	Gourock ... ... ,,		8 5
Gourock... ... ,,	—	8 46	—	Craigendoran... ... ,,		8G 40
Wemyss Bay ... ,,	—	—	9 33			
STEAMER				**TRAIN**		
Craigendoran ... lve.	8R 40	—	—	Gourock ... ... lve.	8 23	—
Gourock... ... ,,	—	—	—	Craigendoran... ... ,,	—	9 4
Dunoon ... ... ,,	—	8 55	—	Dumbarton (Cen.) ... arr.	—	9 17
Wemyss Bay ... ,,	—	9 15	—	Singer ... ... ,,	—	9 28
			9 40	Greenock (West) ... ,,	8 30	—
Rothesay... ... ,,		10 15		Greenock (Cen.) ... ,,	8 33	—
Largs ... ... ,,		10 45		Port Glasgow... ... ,,	8 40	—
Millport (Keppel P.) ,,		11 0		Paisley (Gilmour St.) ... ,,	9 1	—
Brodick ... ... ,,		11 55		Glasgow (Queen St.) ... ,,	—	9 48
		p.m.		Glasgow (Central) ... ,,	9 20	—
Ayr ... ... arr.		1 15				

DAY RETURN FARES TO

From	Ayr 2nd Class Rail	Brodick 2nd Class Rail	From	Ayr	Brodick
Dumbarton (Cen.) ...	19/7	17/4	Brodick	9/9	—
Glasgow (Cen.) ...	21/9	20/-	Craigendoran ...	17/3	15/-
Glasgow (Qu. St.) ...	21/9	20/-	Dunoon	15/6	14/-
Greenock (Cen.) ...	17/8	16/5	Gourock	17/3	15/-
Greenock (West) ...	17/8	16/5	Largs	11/9	9/6
Paisley (Gil. St.) ...	20/11	19/3	Millport	11/9	8/6
Port Glasgow ...	18/10	17/2	Rothesay ...	14/6	11/9
Singer ...	21/3	19/-	Wemyss Bay ...	15/6	14/-

First Class Rail Tickets also obtainable via Gourock or Wemyss Bay.

A—Change at Port Glasgow. G—Change at Gourock. R—Change at Rothesay.
U—Upper Greenock Station.
The tickets are valid on the date for which issued.
Brodick Castle—Open to the public from 1.0 p.m. to 5.0 p.m.

BURNS COUNTRY
The Western S.M.T. Company's Buses will await the arrival of the above Steamer at
AYR Harbour to convey passengers to and from Burns' Cottage and Monument,
Auld Brig o' Doon and Alloway Kirkyard, etc.
Return Fare 1/5. Tickets to be obtained on Steamer

enty-Nine

In the 1950s and 1960s a popular sailing was the Friday trip by the *Duchess of Hamilton* from Gourock to Ayr, with the 1964 timings seen here.

Ayr was not only a harbour for pleasure steamers, but a busy commercial harbour, as seen in this postcard view posted in August 1914. To the left is the entrance to the Griffin Dock and the North Harbour, which at that time was reached by a lock gate, and to the right Compass Pier, used today by *Waverley*.

A postcard view of yachts in Ayr harbour taken from the shipyard showing *Waverley's* berth at Compass Pier as it was a century or more ago.

The Esplanade and adjoining beach at Ayr are little changed in over a century.

Visitors to Ayr by steamer could alternatively head for the shops in the Sandgate, seen here in a postcard view posted in September 1903 ...

... and also in the High Street, seen here in a postcard view, posted in April 1913.

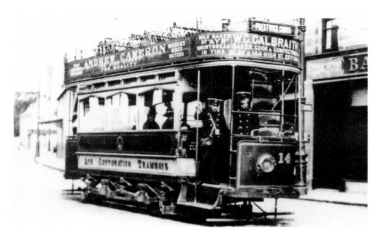

It was possible to take a tram north to Prestwick.

Prestwick boasted a large open air swimming pool, seen here in an illustration from a 1937 guide book.

Passengers could also take a tram south to Alloway, seen here passing Rozelle Wood.

Burns' cottage, the main attraction at Alloway, with a tram in the background. The Ayr tramway network closed in December 1931.

Visitors to Alloway could also see the Auld Brig O' Doon, made famous in Robert Burns' poem 'Tam O' Shanter'.

Above: Also in Alloway is the Burns Monument, built in 1831.

Below left: In 1934 the *Queen Mary* made some late season Friday sailings to Girvan from the upper Firth and the Arran piers of Brodick, Lamlash and Whiting Bay, as in this handbill from 13 September 1934.

Below right: Occasional special sailings were given to Girvan in the inter-war years, like this one by the *Queen Empress* on 11 July 1934, which was also offered from the East Arran Piers. She sailed to Girvan every year until her sale to the Caledonian Steam Packet in 1935.

Above: Juno arriving at Girvan in her GSWR colours.

Below: Waverley continues to sail to Girvan on her Monday sailings from Glasgow. She is seen there in her pre-rebuild condition on a Clyde River Steamer Club excursion sailing on 24 April 1993.

You could also hire rowing boats from Girvan, as seen in this postcard view posted in April 1906.

There was a steamer service from Girvan to Ailsa Craig to land, with the steamer *Ailsa*, which was on the route from building in 1906 until 1924, seen here departing from Girvan.

To STRANRAER,

On TUESDAYS, 11th and 18th AUGUST,

as under:—　　　　　　　　　RETURN JOURNEY.

		a.m.				p.m.
Largs,	dep.	9 0	Stranraer,	dep.	3 30
Millport (Keppel Pier),	,,	9 15	Ayr,	,,	6 10
Ardrossan,	,,	9 55	Troon,	,,	6 40
Troon,	,,	10 30	Ardrossan,	,,	7 20
Ayr,	,,	11 5	Millport (Keppel Pier),	,,	8 0
Stranraer,	arr. abt.	1 45p	Largs,	arr. abt.	8 15

RETURN FARES.

	SALOON.	STEERAGE.
From LARGS or MILLPORT,	3/	2/
,, ARDROSSAN, TROON, or AYR,	2/6	2/

Above: Stranraer saw very occasional sailings from the upper Firth, as in this extract from the GSWR steamer timetable for 1896, for two trips by *Neptune* from Largs.

Left: A handbill for cruises from Princes Pier, Gourock and Dunoon to Stranraer by *King Edward* on 3 August 1928.

NEW SPECIAL EXCURSION

(WEATHER FAVOURABLE)

On FRIDAY, 3rd AUGUST

BY TURBINE STEAMER

"King Edward"

— TO —

STRANRAER

(Allowing about 1 hour on Shore)

From	Depart	Due back
PRINCES PIER	8-30 a.m.	8-20 p.m.
GOUROCK	8-40 a.m.	8-5 p.m.
DUNOON	9-0 a.m.	7-50 p.m.

Stranraer arrive 1-45 p.m.

Passengers will have an excellent view of BUTE, CUMBRAE, ARRAN, AILSA CRAIG, the AYRSHIRE and GALLOWAY COAST and LOCH RYAN

CHEAP DAY FARES:

Saloon 6/-; Fore-Saloon 4/-

The Island of Bute

Right: Traditionally, the main route to Rothesay was from Craigendoran or Gourock via Dunoon and Innellan, as in this photo of the fan-boards on *Jeanie Deans c.* 1960. The Health and Safety brigade would have a fit if they saw this boy doing that nowadays.

Below: Rothesay Pier, prior to the building of the new pier buildings in 1885, with an unidentified paddle steamer across the end, from a lantern slide.

Argyle (1866) moored across the end of the pier, in a shot taken prior to 1885.

Rothesay Pier from the east in a photographic view taken between 1885 and 1890, with *Athole* across the eastern end of the pier, *Columba* about to berth, and the Wemyss Bay steamer *Adela* berthed at the western end of the pier.

Rothesay's Pier Head with street traders, and the funnel of the GSWR's *Atalanta* peeping over the pier buildings.

Rothesay Pier with the 1891 *Lord of the Isles* berthing at the east end and the GSWR's *Neptune* or *Mercury* berthed farther along the pier. There is again a large crowd on the pier. This is from a postcard posted in August 1905; part of the message reads 'Every place is blocked with folk'. The person tinting the postcard has omitted to colour the funnel of the GSWR steamer.

Rothesay Pier from the east in a Tuck's 'Oilette' postcard from the 'Clyde Watering Places' series. *Ivanhoe* is berthed as the east end, a Caledonian Steam Packet steamer across the West end, and *Columba* is heading off towards the Kyles of Bute.

Another Tucks 'Oilette' postcard of Rothesay Pier from the east, this time from the *Bute N.B.* series. Two paddle steamers are berthed, which owe more to the imagination of the artist than to reality.

Rothesay (West)

A much less crowded Rothesay Pier from the east with *Columba* and *Duchess of Fife* berthed across the western end of the pier and another unidentified steamer toward the western end of the pier.

A similar view from 1937 with *Duchess of Hamilton*, *Kenilworth* and *Jupiter*. By this time the trees have grown in the foreground.

A 1950s postcard view from the same viewpoint with *St Columba* (with one funnel removed in the studio), an *ABC* car ferry, and a *Maid* berthed. The photo has obviously been retouched after the withdrawal of *St Columba* in 1958, to make her superficially resemble *Duchess of Montrose* or *Duchess of Hamilton*.

The Albert Pier at Rothesay, mainly used as a cargo pier, in the 1960s with the puffer *Stormlight* berthed.

Marchioness of Breadalbane departing from the berth across the eastern end of Rothesay Pier for Innellan, Dunoon and Gourock in the 1890s.

Queen Empress seen berthed at Rothesay between 1937 and 1939, with *Juno* arriving at the pier, taken from *Queen Mary II*.

Duchess of Fife at Rothesay Pier in an early colour photo.

Lady of the Isles, formerly *Lord of the Isles* of 1877, at Rothesay during her brief spell on the Clyde between May and August 1903 after she had returned from her time on the Thames. She broke down on 29 August 1903 after her boiler failed, and never sailed again.

Maid of Cumbrae, dressed overall, at Rothesay in the mid-1960s with *Lochfyne* departing the far end of the pier.

Caledonia at Rothesay in the 1960s with passengers queuing on the pier, waiting to get aboard.

Sir Robert McAlpine's *Bournemouth Queen* arriving at Rothesay from Ardyne in 1974, prior to her being renamed *Queen of Scots* in July 1975.

Duchess of Hamilton at Rothesay, seen from a self-drive motorboat in 1964.

Talisman at Rothesay in her 1936 to 1938 colour scheme with a grey hull.

Eagle III and *Juno* berthed at Rothesay between 1937 and 1939. Neither would return to service after the ensuing war, the former being unfit for reconditioning after the conflict, and the latter being bombed on 20 March 1941 in the Surrey Commercial Docks in London, while serving as a minesweeper.

A crowd of passengers in all their Edwardian finery on Rothesay pier with MacBrayne's *Iona* berthed to the left, from a postcard view posted in August 1905.

Rothesay Pier.

RELIABLE SERIES. R 1804

Rothesay Pier, giving a good view of the pier buildings, in a postcard view posted in 1907.

Rothesay Pier from the east with the NB steamer *Kenilworth* off the east end of the pier, MacBrayne's *Columba* about to berth, and the *Marchioness of Breadalbane* lying across the west end of the pier with a large crowd of passengers on the pier. Rothesay was, and remains, the most popular of the Clyde resorts. The 1885 pier buildings with the clock tower can be seen.

Buchanan's *Eagle III* berthing at the west end of Rothesay pier in a pre-1914 sepia postcard view.

The inner harbour at Rothesay in an Edwardian postcard view with a puffer berthed, seen looking from the pier.

A similar view in the other direction, looking towards the pier with a puffer in the inner harbour, a small steam yacht inside the pier, and a NB Paddle steamer at the pier.

Bandstand, Rothesay

A large bandstand was a feature of the gardens on the Esplanade to the west of Rothesay Pier, seen here with the CSP's *Duchess of Fife* and another unidentified steamer as the pier.

The Esplanade at Rothesay with *Isle of Bute* leaving the end of the pier, and *Columba* or *Iona* berthed at the pier.

This view of Rothesay Pier from Chapel Hill with the church spire in the foreground, was a popular subject for postcards. This is a London & North Western Railway official postcard, unusually with no steamers at the pier or in the bay.

Rothesay from Chapel Hill with *Iona* having just left the pier for the Kyles of Bute, Tarbert and Ardrishaig.

Rothesay pier from the west with *Strathmore* at the inner berth, the turbine steamer *King Edward* departing, and the turbine steamer *Queen Alexandra* of 1902 arriving, in a view taken between 1902 and 1907.

The Children's Corner on the beach below the Esplanade at Rothesay photographed between 1937 and 1939 with *Saint Columba* departing and *Juno* berthed at the pier.

Rothesay Illuminations and fireworks was a favourite destination for evening cruises in pre-war years. This is a postcard view of the firework display posted in August 1932.

In 1882 a 4-foot gauge horse tramway was built from Rothesay to Port Bannatyne. One of the cars is seen here at the Guildford Square terminus at Rothesay, opposite the pier entrance, in a postcard view posted in September 1902.

An open-sided Rothesay horse tram. Although the board says Port Bannatyne &
Ettrick Bay, it was not until some three years after the demise of the horse trams that
the tramway reached Ettrick Bay, passengers up to then being expected to walk there
from Port Bannatyne.

In March 1902 the horse tramway was closed, converted to 3 foot 6 inch gauge
and electrified. It reopened in August 1902 and in July 1905 a two and a half mile
extension to Ettrick Bay, on the other side of the island, was opened. Three electric
trams are to be seen in this postcard view of Guildford Square, Rothesay, posted in
June 1908.

An electric tram in Victoria Street, Rothesay, in a postcard view posted in August 1905.

The route from Port Bannatyne to Ettrick Bay was rural, with the trams running on a reserved track.

Open toast-rack trams were also operated, like this one seen at Ettrick Bay.

The tramway was sold to Western Scottish Motor Traction (Western SMT) in 1932 and was closed in September 1936, being replaced by buses. The rails were lifted soon after although some stretches of tram track are still in situ in the bus garage at Ardbeg. This is a 1950s view of Guildford Square with seven Western SMT buses to be seen.

A street view in Rothesay entitled 'Post Office. Rothesay.' The Post Office is beyond the shops on the right hand side of the street.

Craigmore Pier was less than a mile out of Rothesay and served the south-eastern suburbs of the Bute capital. It is seen here with a NB steamer arriving and another behind her.

Waverley of 1899 departing Craigmore in a postcard view posted in August 1913.

Craigmore, with the former GSWR paddle steamer *Mercury* in post-1925 colours berthed, half-hidden by foliage and building, and a laid-up cargo steamer anchored off-shore, in a postcard view posted in July 1943, in which the writer states that he has been on a two hour trip up the Kyles of Bute.

A few miles south of Craigmore is the village of Kerrycroy, built by the wife of the Second Marquis of Bute to house the estate workers at Mount Stuart house.

Further south on the eastern shore of Bute is the village of Kilchattan Bay with its pier, seen here in 1919 with two steamers berthed.

Kilchattan Bay pier in the early 1950s with *Talisman*. The pier closed in 1955.

North of Rothesay is the village of Port Bannatyne, which marks the end of Rothesay's urban area, mainly ribbon development along the coast road. It had a pier, seen here in 1919 with Williamson-Buchanan's *Isle of Skye*, ex-*Madge Wildfire* and a group of demurely dressed ladies considering whether to go down to the beach.

The village of Port Bannatyne in a photograph published in 1895. Note the children playing on the beach and the boat-hirer's hut on the shoreline.

The little steamer *Saga*, built in 1893 for service to the South Isles of Orkney, and later operating from Cromarty to Invergordon, laid up at Port Bannatyne stone jetty in the 1930s.

Island of Great Cumbrae

MILLPORT PIER AND LITTLE CUMBRAE

Millport (Old Pier) was the main gateway to the Cumbrae Islands. *Marchioness of Breadalbane* is seen there in a pre-1914 postcard view.

THE PIER, MILLPORT.

Glen Rosa, in post-1925 colours, seen here arriving at Millport.

Ashton, one of the two small motor vessels that maintained the service from Largs to Millport from 1952 until 1964, seen here departing from Millport (Old Pier).

Ashton and her sister *Leven* passing off the Cumbrae coast, with the Hunterston peninsula in the background prior to the building of the nuclear power stations there.

The former Kyle-Kyleakin ferry *Lochalsh* moored along the side of the pier at Millport, with *Maid of Argyll* moored across the end of the pier in 1965-1969 livery.

The main street in Millport, overlooking the sea, in a postcard view posted in 1907.

The harbour at Millport in an Edwardian postcard view.

A feature of the shoreline in Millport is the garishly painted Alligator Rock.

The beach at Millport on another from Tuck's 'Oilette' Clyde Watering Places series.

Keppel Pier, round the corner from Millport, facing the Ayrshire mainland, in a Tucks' 'Rapholette' postcard view posted in September 1907, with a CSP steamer berthed there.

Keppel Pier with the Caledonian Steam Packet's paddle steamer *Duchess of Hamilton* berthed, in a pre-1914 view.

The turbine *Duchess of Hamilton* berthed at Millport (Keppel) on 5 September 1970, on a Clyde River Steamer Club charter. Keppel was very much the subsidiary pier on Cumbrae, being mainly used for the Campbeltown service.

The Island of Arran

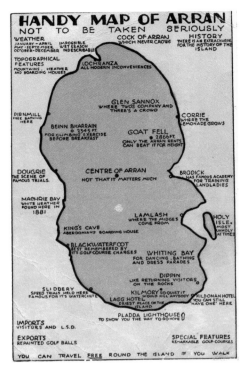

HANDY MAP OF ARRAN
NOT TO BE TAKEN SERIOUSLY

WEATHER
JANUARY - APRIL IMPOSSIBLE
MAY - SEPTEMBER WET SEASON
OCTOBER - DECEMBER INDESCRIBABLE

COCK OF ARRAN
WHICH NEVER CROWS

HISTORY
THERE IS AN EXTRA CHARGE
FOR THE HISTORY OF THE
ISLAND

TOPOGRAPHICAL
FEATURES
MOUNTAINS; HEATHER
AND BOARDING HOUSES

LOCHRANZA
ALL MODERN INCONVENIENCES

GLEN SANNOX
WHERE TWO'S COMPANY AND
THREE'S A CROWD

CORRIE
WHERE THE
LEMONADE GROWS

PIRNMILL
FREE BATHING
HERE

BEINN BHARRAIN
2345 FT
FOR CLIMBING EXERCISE
BEFORE BREAKFAST

GOAT FELL
2866FT
ONLY THE ARRAN RENTS
CAN BEAT IT FOR HEIGHT

DOUGRIE
THE SCENE OF
FAMOUS TRIALS

CENTRE OF ARRAN
NOT THAT IT MATTERS MUCH

BRODICK
HAS FAMOUS ACADEMY
FOR TRAINING
LANDLADIES

MACHRIE BAY
WHITE HEATHER
FOUND HERE IN
1881

LAMLASH
WHERE THE MIDGES
COME FROM

HOLY
ISLE
MOST
UNHOLY
AT TIMES

KING'S CAVE
ABERDONIANS' BOARDING HOUSE

BLACKWATERFOOT
BEST REMEMBERED BY
IT'S GOLF COURSE CHARGES

WHITING BAY
FOR DANCING, BATHING
AND DRESS PARADES

DIPPIN
LIKE RETURNING VISITORS
ON THE ROCKS

SLIDDERY
SPEED TRIALS HELD HERE
FAMOUS FOR IT'S WATERCHUTE

KILMORY SO QUIET IT
WOULD KILL ANYBODY

KILDONAN HOTEL
YOU CAN STILL
HAVE ONE HERE

LAGG HOTEL
DRIEST PLACE ON THE
ISLAND

PLADDA LIGHTHOUSE
TO SHOW YOU THE WAY TO GO HOME

IMPORTS
VISITORS AND L.S.D.

EXPORTS
REPAINTED GOLF BALLS

SPECIAL FEATURES
REMARKABLE GOLF COURSES

YOU CAN TRAVEL FREE ROUND THE ISLAND IF YOU WALK

Left: A Handy map of Arran, not to be taken seriously. This postcard seems to have been produced in the 1930s and reprinted continuously until the 1960s or later.

Below: Lochranza, at the North of Arran was a call by the Campbeltown steamers. *Davaar* is seen arriving at the pier in her two-funnelled form prior to 1903.

A crowded *Queen Alexandra* of 1912 at Lochranza Pier, in a postcard view posted in 1928.

Lochranza has an ancient ruined castle, originally built in the thirteenth century.

Corrie was a ferry call by the Arran via the Kyles steamer. The GSWR's *Jupiter* is seen being tended there by small rowing boats *c.* 1912 with some passengers embarking on a larger boat at the opening of the aft end of the sponson.

An unidentified mid-Victorian steamer is seen here departing from Brodick in an old engraving.

The GSWR paddle steamer *Glen Sannox* berthed at Brodick Pier. She maintained the service from Ardrossan from building in 1892 until 1909.

Duchess of Hamilton departs from the original wrought-iron pier at Brodick in a photograph published in 1895.

Caledonian Steam Packet turbine *Duchess of Argyll* in 1910-1914 condition at Brodick Pier with a fleet of torpedo boats in the bay.

The turbine *Glen Sannox* berthed at Brodick in a 1920s or 1930s postcard view.

The car ferry *Glen Sannox* departs Brodick on 18 May 1968 dressed overall for a Clyde Steamer Club charter round Bute.

Brodick Beach and the mountain of Goat Fell in a Valentine's Art Colour postcard from the 1930s.

The mountains of Arran are a major attraction for visitors to the island, as seen in this postcard view of Glen Rosa.

Lamlash was the destination for early steamers in Arran, prior to the building of Brodick pier in 1872. Here, *Ivanhoe* is lying off and *Guinevere* is at Lamlash pier in the early 1880s.

Channel Fleet, Holy Isle, Lamlash.

RELIABLE SERIES.R163.

Lamlash was used by naval ships as an anchorage. Here the Channel Fleet lies in the shelter of Holy Isle in an early postcard view.

A stone jetty survives at Lamlash, and *Balmoral* called there in 1994 on a CRSC charter. This was the first call at the stone jetty. The final call at the pier was made in 1955 by *Duchess of Hamilton*.

Whiting Bay, the third of the East Arran piers, had the longest pier in the Firth of Clyde. This postcard shows the Bay during the inter-war years, with *Glen Sannox* berthed and a line-up of taxis and a bus awaiting passengers.

The village of Whiting Bay seen from the pier in a postcard view posted in September 1906.

Other Clyde Islands

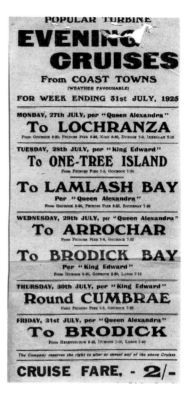

One Tree Island, Eilean Dearg on Loch Riddon, was another destination for non-landing evening cruises, like the one advertised here for 28 July 1930 from Princes Pier and Gourock by *King Edward*. It is said that it was given that name by the steamer operator because it had a single tree growing on it.

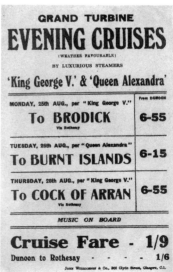

The Burnt Islands, the three small islands of Eilean Mor, Eilean Fraoich and Eilean Buidhe, situated in the Kyles of Bute, were a favourite destination for non-landing evening cruises, as in that advertised here for 26 August 1930 by *Queen Alexandra* from Dunoon.

The GSWR's *Jupiter* making a ferry call at Kings Cross, at the south end of Lamlash Bay, with Edwardian ladies in all their finery, complete with a couple of dogs and a packing case, waiting to board.

Skate Island in Loch Fyne was the destination for non-landing afternoon cruises by *Queen Mary* in 1933, and again towards the end of her career in 1969. This handbill gives details of a trip on 21 September 1933 from Dunoon, Rothesay, Craigmore, Largs and Millport (Old Pier), returning via Millport (Keppel Pier).

Horse Island, off Ardrossan, was another evening cruise destination by *King Edward*, advertised here to sail there from Helensburgh on 14 August 1925.

Yet another evening cruise destination was Holy Isle, where the 'luxurious steamer' *Queen Alexandra* was advertised to sail to on 22 July 1934 from Dunoon, Rothesay, Largs and Millport (Old Pier) with a Young's Bus connection from Kilbirnie, Lochwinnoch, Paisley, and Glasgow.

EVERY FRIDAY (5th June to 11th September)
By T.S. "DUCHESS OF HAMILTON"

TO ARRAN COAST and ROUND HOLY ISLE

Leaving Ayr Harbour at 1.45 p.m.   CRUISE **6/6** FARE   Arriving back at 4.0 p.m.

When *Duchess of Hamilton* was lying at Ayr on her Friday trip from the upper Firth she undertook an afternoon cruise round Holy Isle. Following the move of *Caledonia* to Craigendoran in 1965, this was the only cruise offered from Ayr.

Ailsa berthed at the slipway at Ailsa Craig *c.* 1911, disembarking passengers from Girvan.